Riches of the Earth

Wool

Irene Franck and David Brownstone

GROLIER

An imprint of Scholastic Library Publishing
Danbury, Connecticut

Credits and Acknowledgments

abbreviations: t (top), b (bottom), l (left), r (right), c (center)

Image credits: Agricultural Research Service Library: 21; Art Resource: 15 (Réunion des Musées Nationaux/ Jean Schomans), 17t (Newark Museum, Gift of the Cyrus O. Baker Estate), 17b (Werner Forman Archive), 18 (Erich Lessing); Friends of the Citadel Society (Halifax, Nova Scotia): 26; Getty Images/PhotoDisc/PhotoLink: 1b (S. Solum), 20 (H. Wiesenhofer); National Aeronautics and Space Administration (NASA): 1t and running heads; Photo Researchers, Inc.: 3 (Barry Lopez), 4 (Ed Michaels), 5 (Alison Wright), 6 (Elisabeth Weiland), 7 (Science Photo Library), 10r (Tom McHugh), 12tl (Jany Sauvanet), 12tr (A. B. Joyce), 12cl (George Holton), 12cr (Fletcher & Baylis), 12b (Holt Studios International/Nigel Cattlin), 22r and 23 (Bill Bachman), 25 (Stephen Saks), 29 (Brian Yarvin); Rudi Schreiber: 22l, 27; U.S. Department of Agriculture: 8 and 9 (Ken Hammond); Woodfin Camp & Associates: 11 and 24 (Eastcott/Momatiuk), 13 (Robert Frerck), 19 and 28 (Katsuyoshi Tanaka). Authors' Archives: 16. Original image drawn for this book by K & P Publishing Services: 14.

Our thanks to Joe Hollander, Phil Friedman, and Laurie McCurley at Scholastic Library Publishing; to photo researchers Susan Hormuth, Robin Sand, and Robert Melcak; to copy editor Michael Burke; and to the librarians throughout the northeastern library network, in particular to the staff of the Chappaqua Library—director Mark Hasskarl; the expert reference staff, including Martha Alcott, Michele J. Capozzella, Maryanne Eaton, Catherine Paulsen, Jane Peyraud, Paula Peyraud, and Carolyn Reznick; and the circulation staff, headed by Barbara Le Sauvage—for fulfilling our wide-ranging research needs.

Published 2003 by Grolier
Division of Scholastic Library Publishing
Old Sherman Turnpike
Danbury, Connecticut 06816

For information address the publisher:
Scholastic Library Publishing, Grolier Division
Old Sherman Turnpike, Danbury, Connecticut 06816

© 2003 Irene M. Franck and David M. Brownstone

All rights reserved. Except for use in a review, no part of this book may be reproduced, stored in a retrieval system, or transmitted in any form, or by any means, electronic or mechanical, including photocopying, recording, or otherwise, without prior permission of Scholastic Library Publishing.

Library of Congress Cataloging-in-Publication Data

Franck, Irene M.
    Wool / Irene Franck and David Brownstone.
      p. cm. -- (Riches of the earth ; v. 16)
    Summary: Provides information about wool and its importance in everyday life.
    Includes bibliographical references and index.
    ISBN 0-7172-5730-4 (set : alk. paper) -- ISBN 0-7172-5728-2 (vol. 16 : alk paper)
      1. Wool--Juvenile literature [1. Wool.] I. Brownstone, David M. II. Title.

TS1547.F73 2003
677'.31--dc21
                                                        2003044087

Printed in the United States of America

Designed by K & P Publishing Services

Contents

Wool— Warmth and Comfort

If you want to keep warm, one of the best fabrics to wear is wool, as in this boy's hat, scarf, and mittens. Wool absorbs moisture, so if it becomes wet it becomes even heavier and warmer.

People have been wearing woolen clothing for at least 10,000 years. Back in the days before anyone knew how to spin or weave wool into clothing, humans wore sheepskins with the wool still attached to protect them from the wind and cold. Later people learned how to remove a sheep's wool without harming the sheep, leaving it to grow more wool. They also learned to spin and weave that wool into many kinds of warm, attractive clothing.

Today millions and millions of people all over the world wear many kinds of woolen clothes, now usually made by massive, tremen-

Wool is used in many kinds of products. This dyed wool drying in the Mexican sun will be woven into carpets.

dously fast machines in huge textile mills. We now know how to make clothes from the wool of not just sheep but also camels, angora and cashmere goats, angora rabbits, alpacas, llamas, and vicuñas. We even know how to make clothes out of the wool of the musk ox.

We also have many more kinds of woolen clothes now than were known for most of the last 10,000 years. Today we make and wear everything from a baby's soft, warm lamb's-wool sweater to flame-resistant clothes worn by automobile racers. We wear woolen sweaters, coats, caps, jackets, linings, suits,

dresses, underwear, socks, and other handknit and handwoven clothes of all kinds. Beyond clothes, wool is used to make many other things, including carpets from many countries, tapestries and other wall hangings, sleeping bags, and furniture coverings.

Yet underneath all the machines and all the variety of woolen products, there may be less change than there seems. Long ago people learned that wool was the best known clothing material for many purposes and that wool also had many other fine qualities (see p. 15).

This is a Shetland sheep heavy with wool before it has been cut off. As in human hairs, the cells are dead except for those at the very base of the hair. As these cells continue to grow, they push the dead cells out and make the hair longer.

What Is Wool?

Wool is the hair of sheep and several other animals. By far the largest amount of the world's wool comes from the fleece (coat of hair) of sheep.

When you look at sheep hairs through a microscope, you see that they are very thin threadlike fibers. Depending on the kind of sheep they come from, the hairs range from one inch to 14 inches long. Like cotton and silk fibers, wool fibers are much longer than they are thick. However, cotton and silk fibers are much thinner than even the finest sheep's hair. During the wool manufacturing process, these sheep hair fibers are first made into yarn and then woven or knit into cloth.

All wool fibers have some natural waves (*crimps*) in them, and the best wools are those that have the most waves. The number of crimps depends on the kinds of sheep the hairs are taken from. These can range from three crimps per inch for the lowest quality wools to 30 crimps per inch for the highest.

Wools with many waves in their fibers have excellent elastic (stretching) qualities. They also hang together (cohere) well and have the most bulk (size). These are all qualities that give wool increased strength and help it to hold its shape and drape (hang) well. In addition, wools with many crimps are easier to gather into long strands called *slivers*, for purposes of spinning and weaving (see p. 24).

All wool, whether from sheep or other animals, is made of *keratin*. Made of carbon, hydrogen, nitrogen, oxygen, and sulfur, keratin is a

Like most animal hairs (including human ones), wool hairs have tiny overlapping scales, as you can see in this highly magnified section of a Shetland wool sweater, from the Shetland Islands north of Scotland.

protein, a kind of chemical compound (mixed material) that is part of all living matter. Keratin is a tough protein, which makes up the hair, nails, hooves, and horns of many animals, as well as human hair and nails.

Sheep's wool today is usually white and soft all the way through. That was not always so. In ancient times sheep's coats were much rougher, and only the underside of the fleece was soft. Colors varied, too. Sheep's wool was often brown, black, or a mixture of several colors. Over the centuries sheep farmers helped produce today's soft, white fleece by *selective breeding*—that is, by choosing to breed those sheep that had desirable light-colored or white fleece.

Qualities of Wool

Most of all, wool is warm and light and holds its warmth extremely well. Wool fibers are very resilient—that is, they bounce back to their original shape after being

This woman is showing her granddaughter the long hair on her Churro sheep near Ganado on the Navajo Reservation in Arizona.

This rancher is holding two batches of wool in his hands. The one on the right has much longer fibers than the one on the left.

crushed or bent—so that they tend to hold the warm air trapped within their fibers. Wool is a poor conductor of heat—that is, it doesn't allow heat to pass through it very easily—so the fibers themselves tend to hold heat. Wool fibers tend to hold moisture, so that when wet, wool even becomes somewhat heavier, denser, and warmer.

Wool also holds its appearance quite well, for it naturally resists wrinkling and resumes its original shape easily during and after wear-ing. Wool is also easily combined with several other fabrics, including cotton and silk.

Kinds of Sheep

More than 1 billion sheep in the world today produce almost 6 billion pounds of wool each year. There are approximately 200 sheep breeds and mixtures of breeds. Some kinds of sheep are bred wholly or mostly for their wool, others for their meat (mutton), and some for both wool and mutton.

Merino sheep are prized above all others for the quality of their wool. As early as 2,000 years ago, Merinos were being bred in Spain. The Spanish government tried to keep them and their great quality and value solely for Spain. However, over many centuries Merinos spread slowly to other European countries and then in several varieties throughout the world.

Merino wool fibers originally were somewhat short, only one to three inches long. However, they have as many as 30 crimps per inch, far more than other kinds of sheep, and are now one of the most favored of wool fibers. In addition, some new varieties of Merino sheep have fibers up to five inches long.

Merinos have been bred to live very successfully in other parts of the world, most notably in Australia, New Zealand, South America, and South Africa. In France, the Rambouillet became a very successful Merino breed. Mixed breeds that include Merinos have helped improve the quality of wool produced throughout the world.

Many other breeds of sheep, some of them originally British, also produce high-quality wool used in clothing. Among them are Britain's Hereford, Blackface, and Southdown breeds. Somewhat coarser wools, but still often used in clothing, are produced by breeds with fibers as much as 18 inches long, such as Cheviot and Shetland sheep.

The Karakul breed of sheep originated in Central Asia but has since spread around the world. The coats of very young Karakuls are sometimes called *Persian lamb*.

This angora rabbit from New Zealand is being clipped by hand for its valuable hair, used to make soft, cuddly angora sweaters and other clothes.

A few breeds, such as the Navajo and Karakul, produce tough, coarse wool used mainly for rugs and carpets.

Other Kinds of Wool

Several kinds of wools are made of the hair of animals other than sheep. In the wool trade these are called *specialty wools*, like the ones described below.

Mohair, made of the hair of the *angora goat*, is produced mainly in South Africa and the United States. It is one of the most widely used specialty wools. Because it is very smooth and strong and holds its shape well, it is much used in hand-knitting, rugs and carpets, and draperies.

Angora is the warm, light, white, silky hair of the *angora rabbit*. It is used mainly in high-quality sweaters and other kinds of clothing.

Camel's hair is a very warm, lightweight tan wool made from the hair of the *Bactrian camel* (the Asian camel with two humps, rather than the one-hump Arabian camel). This hair is used in high-quality, warm clothing.

Alpaca is the strong, lightweight, water-resistant hair of the alpaca, a South American member of the camel family. It is used mainly as a warm, high-quality lining material.

Llama is the soft, high-quality hair of the llama, another South American member of the camel family. It is used mainly for clothing, as well as for handmade rugs.

Vicuña is the very rare, soft, fine, much-prized hair of the vicuña, still another South American member of the camel family. The vicuña is today a rare and endangered species, so vicuña wool has become tremendously expensive.

Cashmere, produced in southern and eastern Asia, is the very soft hair of the inner coat of the *cashmere goat*. It is a very soft, warm, easily damaged wool. Very high quality and very expensive, this wool is used in sweaters and other clothing.

Quiviut is the very soft, warm, light hair of the undercoat of the *musk ox*, found in Canada and Alaska.

Llama

Angora goat

Bactrian camel

Musk ox

Alpaca

Beyond sheep, several other kinds of animals yield specialty wools. These include the Bactrian camel, the llama, the alpaca, the musk ox, and the angora goat (source of mohair).

In some rural parts of the world, people still weave woolen cloth by hand, like this woman weaving a warm blanket in the chilly highlands of Peru.

Wool around the World

In ancient times wool-producing sheep were raised over a huge area that extended from Iraq to India. Shepherds and their flocks of sheep were found in many countries, among them what are now Iraq, Syria, Israel, Palestine, Lebanon, Iran, Afghanistan, Pakistan, and India.

Sheep raising later spread throughout much of Europe and Asia. Growing sheep primarily for their wool followed later. The Romans brought wool production to Britain and to many of the countries of mainland Europe. Wool was also being produced in South America and Central America in ancient times.

However, the main sheep-raising countries today did not even have sheep until the last few centuries. They were only introduced when European colonists arrived.

Today Australia is the world's largest wool-producing country by far, producing almost 30 percent of

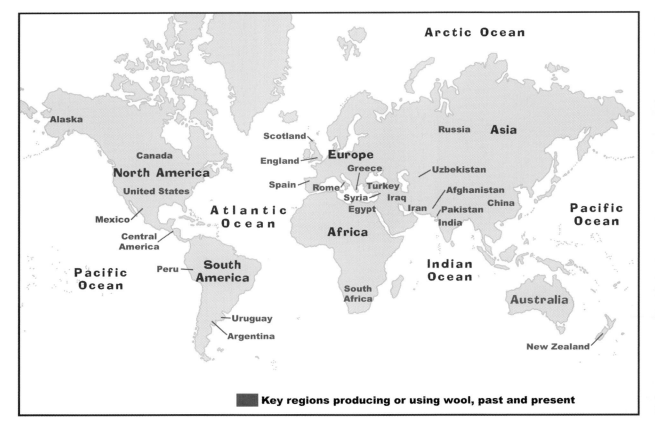

Key regions producing or using wool, past and present

the world's wool. This South Pacific country, which is a whole continent, has the largest Merino sheep population in the world. It produces more than 40 percent of the world's Merino wool, from the Australian variety of the Merino. Very large numbers of Australia's sheep are raised on huge ranches called *stations*. However, sheep are also raised on much smaller ranches by tens of thousands of family farmers.

New Zealand, also in the South Pacific, is the world's second-largest wool-producing country. Like Australia, New Zealand's sheep are raised on both large sheep stations and smaller family farms. Behind Australia and New Zealand in wool production come South Africa, China, Argentina, Uruguay, Russia, and Uzbekistan.

The United States is a major consumer of wool. However, it produces only a little over one percent of the world's supply. Most American high-quality wools are produced by sheep raised in Texas and California. Wools of other qualities are produced in many other states.

This French tapestry dating from about 1500 shows various stages in the working of wool. The man in the center carries the staff traditionally associated with shepherds, who keep the sheep together and safe from harm. The woman at the right is shearing wool, while the one at the left is carding it—that is, combing, straightening, and cleaning it. Tapestries like this were often woven in wool, sometimes combined with silk or cotton.

Wool in History

Sheep and the wool they produce have long played a notable role in human history. The first woolen clothing was probably made of sheepskins taken from wild sheep, which were hunted for their meat. Sheep and goats were domesticated (tamed for human purposes) in the Middle East in what is now Iraq by 8650 B.C., more than 10,650 years ago.

Wool, cotton, silk, linen, and other fabrics are hard to date accurately. That is because they have much shorter lives than stone, iron, diamonds, and many other ancient remnants found by archaeologists. However, archaeologists have found woven cloth remnants, some of them thought to be made of wool at Çatal Hüyük in Anatolia (now Turkey). Those remnants have been dated to about 7000 B.C. to 6400 B.C.—that is, between 9,000 and 8,400 years ago. Woven cloth remnants just as old, some of them also possibly of wool, have been found at other Middle Eastern archaeological sites in what are now Iraq, Turkey, Jordan, and Israel.

By 6,000 years ago (about 4000 B.C.) woolen clothing and other woolen goods were being used throughout the Middle East. By 4,000 years ago (about 2000 B.C.), woolens were being widely traded in the ancient world, in a huge area that stretched from Mesopotamia (now Iraq) to India.

By then the use of woolens had also spread to Europe. Woolen cloth remnants dating back 4,400 years have been found in Switzerland.

In Greek and Roman times, 2,500 to 2,000 years ago, weavers from Egypt to India were creating many kinds of woolens, from the smallest items of clothing to great tapestries (wall hangings). Roman armies brought woolens to Britain and the rest of the Roman Empire more than 2,000 years ago.

Wool has been used for many purposes in many places all over the world, even in places we commonly think of as hot, such as the Middle East. The traditional black tents of the Bedouin, like those shown here in David Roberts's painting of a Bedouin camp at Mt. Sinai in Egypt, were woven from the black hair of goats kept by these desert people.

This blanket, made by the Tlingit people of coastal Alaska, was woven of wool from mountain goats plus cedar bark.

Wool was important in many cultures. Figures like this woman in gold, wrapped in a beautiful wool robe, were often found in the burial sites of the early Incas of Peru. This one dates to the late 1400s or early 1500s.

Wool in the Americas

Wool was being woven into cloth in the Americas as well. At least 2,000 years ago weavers in Peru were using the wool of llamas, alpacas, vicuñas, and other animals to create clothing and several other kinds of woolens.

By 500 A.D., about 1,500 years ago, highly skilled Peruvian weavers were producing heavy woolen tapestries. As artworks these fully equaled many of the tapestries then being produced in Europe. The greatest period of European tapestry weaving came later, starting in the 1200s and 1300s. By then South American and Central American weavers were also producing major tapestry artworks.

Even before modern factories were developed in the late 1700s, spinning and weaving were made much easier by the development of large spinning wheels, like the two in the foreground, and devices that allowed the winding of yarn on many spindles at once (center background). This painting by Isaac Claesz van Swanenburgh, *Workers Spinning and Weaving Wool,* dates from about 1600.

Sheep raising for wool and the wool trade became major European industries in the 1400s and 1500s. In this period Spain's Merino sheep breed spread widely in Europe, and several high-quality Merino varieties were developed. British sheep raisers also began to develop many other breeds of sheep. Some of these breeds would spread throughout the world.

By the 1600s Britain was Europe's leading wool producer. It was also well on its way to developing Europe's leading wool and cotton goods industries. In the 1800s it would become the world's leading manufacturer of woolen and cotton clothing and other wool and cotton goods. Much of the spinning and weaving (see p. 24) was done by individuals working in their own homes or in small workshops.

Modern Times

A tremendous set of changes began in the world of industry during the 1700s. New, far-reaching inventions—most of them created by British inventors—made it possible to change the way the world's goods were produced. Low-cost mass production in ever-larger factories replaced the kind of small-scale home workshop production that had been the rule for thousands of years.

The textile industries, starting with cotton and wool, were the first to see major changes—and those changes would provide models later adopted by many other industries. By the early 1770s such inventors as Richard Arkwright and James Hargreave had developed new, fast, powerful spinning and weaving machines. The new machines needed much more power than earlier spinning and weaving. This power was supplied by James Watt's newly invented steam engine.

The new machines and mass production processes needed far larger numbers of workers and far larger workplaces than the earlier home-production systems. Large factories soon began to replace home workshops.

Britain and America quickly developed the world's first major factory systems, starting with the cotton and wool textile mills of northern England and the then-new United States. Such factory systems would become the main way of manufacturing goods throughout the world's industrial countries. Today's modern industries have developed from these early mills and the factory system they introduced.

Most modern spinning of wool is done by machine. This factory in Peru is spinning alpaca wool to be woven into sweaters.

Sheep often graze in high fields, far from the farmer's house and barns. At shearing time they are driven down from the heights to the shearing barns.

Sheep and Wool

Sheep are raised for two quite different purposes and in two different kinds of places. Sheep raised for their wool—and especially those producing high-quality wool—are *range sheep*. They are born and raised in big flocks (called *bands*) on large sheep ranches and live out on the open range. Flocks of range sheep often run to more than 1,000 ewes (female sheep) and lambs (young sheep). Rams (male sheep) are used mainly for breeding purposes. Except in deep winter, range sheep are constantly on the move. They go from one pasture (group of fields) to another in search of food.

On the other hand, some sheep are raised for their mutton. They generally live in much smaller farm flocks on farms producing several different kinds of products.

Food for Sheep

Sheep eat many kinds of plant foods but no meat. Indeed, they are well known for eating what often seems like almost any and every kind of plant food, right down to the ground.

That was one of the main causes of the long battle—sometimes called the "sheep wars"—in the American West in the late 1800s. Most cattle ranchers at that time tried to keep sheep out of "their" range, claiming that sheep ate up all the grass their cattle needed to survive. Later it became clear that cattle and sheep could live on the same ranges.

As a practical matter, sheep do eat grass, peas, beans, alfalfa, clover, hay, and just about every other green plant they can find out on the range. In winter, when the sheep often need more food than they can get for themselves, sheep raisers add such additional foods as stored hay, corn, cereals, cottonseed oil, corn, oats, wheat, barley, and rye.

In the late 19th-century American West, cattle and sheep ranchers were enemies because they thought the sheep ate up grass needed by the cattle. However, today cattle and sheep often graze together in a *flerd* (a combination of *flock* and *herd*), as here.

Below is a close-up of the comblike powered shearing device used to cut the fleece close to the skin.

This Australian shearer is just finishing shearing a sheep. The pile of wool on the floor has all come from that one sheep.

Wool from Sheep

Sheepshearing—that is, cutting the wool off the sheep—is usually done once a year in the spring. However, it is done twice a year in some warm climates, as in Texas and California, the major American wool-producing states. It is done by expert shearers using large power clippers. These are very much like the electric clippers barbers use in haircuts—and it is normally just as painless for the sheep as haircuts are for people.

Expert traveling sheepshearers usually clip the wool off a sheep in one piece and in as little as three to five minutes. Most experienced shearers can clip 150 to 175 sheep a day, but some go as high as 200 to 225 a day.

Once clipped, the fleece of the sheep becomes *raw wool*. This is rolled and tied into bags or bales, and then sent on to warehouses or woolen mills. There it is prepared for manufacturing into several kinds of cloth and other woolen products.

There are three main kinds of

raw wool. The first is *lamb's wool*. This soft, very high-quality wool is the first wool ever sheared from a young sheep. The second, called *hogget wool*, is the first wool sheared from mature (fully grown) sheep. The third, called *wether wool*, is all the rest of the wool sheared from mature sheep later in their lives.

Another kind of wool, far inferior to the sheared wools, is *pulled wool*. This is wool separated chemically from the skin of sheep that have been killed for their meat. Yet another low-quality kind of wool is *dead wool*, which is the wool of sheep that have died of natural causes.

Recycled wool is also used in wool manufacturing. Some is wool that has been part of earlier woolen products and is now being reused. The rest includes small amounts of unused scrap wool recovered from earlier manufacturing processes.

When it is time to shear the wool, sheep are brought down from the hills to the shearing sheds. There they wait their turn in holding pens, like these Merino sheep in New Zealand.

This modern New Zealand woman is spinning wool in a traditional way, with a foot-operated spinning wheel. This helps her turn the wool in the basket into spun yarn, which is wound around the spindle at the top of the device.

From Wool to Cloth

Today, as for many thousands of years, only a few basically simple tools are used for making woolen yarn and cloth. They are used whether yarn and cloth will in the end become a warm muffler, a sweater, a beautiful Navajo blanket, or a huge, magnificent carpet or tapestry wall covering.

The most basic of these tools is the *spindle*. This started out as a notched stick used for spinning any kind of fiber, including wool, into yarn. The spindle is designed literally to spin and twist wool and other fibers into a yarn of roughly even width. After thousands of years, the idea of the spinning stick was used to invent the spinning wheel. The wheel helped make the spinning process somewhat easier and faster. Both the spindle and the spinning wheel were hand tools worked by individual highly skilled spinners. Today the same spinning spindle has become a big, complicated set of spinning machines in a modern textile mill—but the principle is the same.

The second of these basic tools is the loom, a device used in weaving yarn into cloth. In weaving, the loom holds one set of threads, the *warp* yarns, tight from end to end in the loom. The *filling* (*weft*) yarns run across the first set, usually at right angles, and are pushed into place by the weaver. The cross-threaded warp and weft threads then lock together to make cloth. For thousands of years weavers worked as highly skilled individuals, creating one piece at a time. Many weavers still work on simple looms. However, in our machine age, the loom—like the spindle—has also become a set of big, fast machines in modern textile mills.

The third basic tool for creating cloth is a set of knitting needles. These are used to make cloth by linking yarn together in loops to form a connected body of cloth. Knitting, too, is a highly skilled

This is how a carpet is made by hand in the traditional way, as here in India. Undyed yarn, such as wool or cotton, is often stretched lengthwise. Then other colored yarns, such as wool or silk, are woven to make the beautiful patterns we see.

Whether in their homeland or around the world, Scots have traditionally raised sheep and made wool products. Each clan (family group) has its own special pattern of colors, like the plaid in this piper's uniform—it even covers his bagpipe!

craft. Yet the vast majority of the world's textiles, including woolens, are now produced by much less skilled people in mass-production textile mills.

At the Textile Mill

On arriving at the textile mill, raw wool must be prepared for manufacturing. First it must be sorted

by pulling each fleece apart. Then all the parts of the wool are graded by their quality, according to government-set standards.

The wool is then scoured—that is, cleaned of soil, bits of twigs and leaves, and other impurities. Scouring also separates out the quite valuable *wool fat* (also called *wool grease*). This can amount to anywhere from 20 percent to 80 percent of the weight of raw wool. Purified wool fat yields a substance called *lanolin*. This softens and soothes skin, and so it is widely used in skin creams, cosmetics, and some medicines.

After scouring comes *blending* (mixing). At this stage cheaper grades of wool are added to expensive, high-quality wool to lower costs. Some wools may also be blended with cotton or other fabrics.

At this point wool headed for spinning begins to become two different kinds of yarn. All of the wool goes into *carding*. This process

This pile of wool has just been removed from a sheep. Its greasy look comes from what is called *wool fat*, which is removed during cleaning. The wool fat is processed to make *lanolin* for skin cream and other uses.

straightens out and further cleans the wool. For thousands of years carding was done by hand, as it still is in some parts of the world. Today, however, most wool goes through a carding machine, which also forms the carded wool into soft, ropelike strands called *slivers*.

During the carding process, one kind of wool is prepared so that its yarn will come out somewhat fuzzy and rough, as in most woolen fabrics. This kind of wool goes on directly to be spun into yarn and then woven into cloth.

The second kind of wool is made into *worsted yarn*. During carding

this wool is processed so as to come out straight and smooth. Then it goes through *gilling* and *combing* processes. These are aimed at further cleaning and straightening the wool, while also removing the shorter fibers. This kind of wool then goes through the *drawing* and *roving* processes. These are aimed at thinning, twisting, and hardening the wool so that it can be spun into smooth, flat, strong worsted yarn and then woven into cloth.

Of the several modern mass production ways of spinning wool into yarn, the most common is *ring spinning*. In this process both kinds of

Today most weaving is done by large machines in factories, like those here in the background, which are weaving alpaca sweaters in Peru. However, the finishing work is still done by hand by workers like these.

wool slivers are shaped into their final forms, given their final twist, and wound on *bobbins* (spools for holding spun yarn or thread). Several other modern ways of machine spinning can be used, but all seek only to spin yarn faster, mainly by cutting out some of the steps in the spinning process.

As spinning still depends on the spindle, so weaving still depends on the loom. Indeed, the basic

handmade wools and weaves produced by skilled weavers are not much different from those produced in textile mills.

There are several widely used wool weaves, some called basic and some called fancy. The most used and least expensive is the *plain weave*. This is used in producing by far the greatest body of the world's clothing and other woven goods. The plain weave might also rightly be called a simple weave, for it is cloth produced on a loom by interlacing warp and filling (weft) yarns at right angles to each other. This makes cloth that is as strong and solid as its yarns and the number of times its crosshatched threads meet.

Plain weaves are done in wool, cotton, silk, linen, and every other natural fiber, as well as in many synthetic fabrics. Wool and other fabrics may also be found in fancy weaves, such as wool crepe.

Though people still knit woolen garments by hand, sometimes as a hobby, most woolens are today knitted by factory machines, like this young woman's sweater and matching cap.

Words to Know

alpaca Wool made of hair from the alpaca, a member of the camel family.

angora Wool made of the hair of the angora rabbit.

carding In making YARN, passing wool fibers through a device that straightens and further cleans them, forming SLIVERS.

cashmere Wool made from the soft hair of the inner coat of the cashmere goat.

combing: See GILLING, COMBING, DRAWING, AND ROVING.

dead wool Wool from sheep that have died of natural causes.

drawing: See GILLING, COMBING, DRAWING, AND ROVING.

ewe An adult female sheep.

fiber Any natural or synthetic (human-made) threadlike substance, such as wool, that can be spun into YARN.

filling: See WEFT.

gilling, combing, drawing, and roving In making wool YARN, steps beyond CARDING, which further thin, twist, and harden the SLIVERS; used only in making WORSTED yarn.

hogget wool The first wool sheared from adult sheep.

keratin The natural substance that all kinds of wool (and also human hair) are made of. Keratin is a *protein*, a kind of chemical compound (mixed substance) that is part of all living matter.

knitting Making fabric by linking YARN together in loops.

lamb A young sheep, usually no more than 10 months old.

lamb's wool Soft, high-quality wool, the first ever sheared from a young sheep.

lanolin A skin softener also used in cosmetics and some medicines; a by-product of WOOL FAT.

llama A South American member of the camel family. Its hair is used to make a kind of wool.

loom The basic tool used in WEAVING, which holds the WARP and WEFT YARNS in place as they are cross-threaded to form cloth.

mohair Wool made of the hair of the angora goat.

protein: See KERATIN.

pulled wool Wool separated chemically from the skin of sheep that have been killed for their meat (mutton).

ram An adult male sheep.

range sheep Sheep born and raised in big flocks (*bands*) on large sheep ranches.

recycled wool Reused wool that has been part of earlier wool products or unused scrap wool.

roving: See GILLING, COMBING, DRAWING, AND ROVING.

scouring Cleaning wool of such impurities as soil and leaves, while also separating out the WOOL FAT.

sheep station A large sheep ranch; usually referring to such a ranch in Australia or New Zealand.

sliver A group of wool FIBERS that form a longer strand of wool. After processing, the slivers can be spun into YARN.

spindle: See SPINNING.

spinning Making YARN out of FIBERS by spinning and twisting the fibers into a thread of roughly even width. This can be done by using a hand-operated device such as a *spindle* or a *spinning wheel*, or powerful spinning machines in factories.

spinning wheel: See SPINNING.

vicuña An extremely rare South American member of the camel family. Its hair is used to make a valuable, scarce kind of wool.

warp The lengthwise YARN held in place by a LOOM.

weaving The process of making cloth out of YARN on a LOOM.

weft The crosswise YARN held in place by a LOOM, interlaced with the WARP yarn. Also called *filling*.

wether wool Wool from the second and later shearings of an adult sheep, after HOGGET WOOL.

wool fat A greasy substance found in raw wool, a source of LANOLIN. Also called *wool grease*.

wool grease: See WOOL FAT.

worsted A kind of smooth, flat, strong yarn, formed by GILLING, COMBING, DRAWING, AND ROVING processes. Also the cloth made from such yarn.

yarn A long thread made out of wool or other FIBERS (see SPINNING), which is used to WEAVE, KNIT, or otherwise form fabrics.

On the Internet

The Internet has many interesting sites about wool. The site addresses often change, so the best way to find current addresses is to go to a search site, such as www.yahoo.com. Type in a word or phrase, such as "wool."

As this book was being written, websites about wool included:

http://www.fabrics.net/wool.asp
A section of Fabrics.Net focusing on wool, with information about different kinds of wool and fabrics woven from it.

http://www.llamapaedia.com/wool/wool.html
Llamapaedia: Wool, which offers information about wool fibers, especially llama hair, including definitions and descriptions of processes.

http://www.interlog.com/~gwhite/ttt/tttintro.html
Textiles Through Time, a private website of links relating to textiles.

http://char.txa.cornell.edu/
Art, Design, and Visual Thinking, a site from Cornell University offering information about fibers, yarns, and designs using them.

In Print

Your local library system will have various books on wool. The following is just a sampling of them.

Burnham, Dorothy K. *Warp and Weft*. Toronto: Royal Ontario Museum, 1980.

Corbman, Bernard P. *Textiles: Fiber to Fabric*. New York: McGraw-Hill, 1983.

Gemming, Elizabeth. *Wool Gathering*. New York: Coward, McCann, 1979.

Hecht, Ann. *The Art of the Loom*. New York: Rizzoli, 1989.

Hopkins, Giles. *Wool*. New York: Rinehart, 1953.

Kadolph, Sara J., and Anna L. Langford. *Textiles*. Upper Saddle River, NJ: Prentice-Hall, 1998.

Lasky, Kathryn. *The Weaver's Gift*. New York: Frederick Warne, 1980.

Textiles: 5,000 Years. Jennifer Harris, ed. New York: Harry N. Abrams, 1993.

Van Nostrand's Scientific Encyclopedia, 8th ed., 2 vols. Douglas M. Considine and Glenn D. Considine, eds. New York: Van Nostrand Reinhold, 1995.

Watson, Tom, and Jenny Watson. *Wool*. Hove, Sussex, UK: Wayland, 1980.

Wingate, Isabel B. *Textile Fibers and Their Selection*. Englewood Cliffs, NJ: Prentice-Hall, 1976.

Index